HOLY DONKEYS, I'M OVER 60!

Holy Donkeys, I'm over 60!

Holy Donkeys, I'm over 60!

A guide to help you make the most of your remaining years of life

by Mayson Brooks

I plan on living forever, so far, so good

Tempus Fugit, so Carpe Diem

Chapters
Instructions
Chapter 1: Do the math
Chapter 2: Make a written plan
Chapter 3: Attitude
Chapter 4: Health & Fitness
Chapter 5: Music
Chapter 6: Travel
Chapter 7: Friends
Chapter 8: Sex
Chapter 9: Memories
Chapter 10: Declutter
Chapter 11: Just in case
Chapter 12: D-Day planning
Chapter 13: Once you have passed
Summary
In Closing

Holy Donkeys, I'm over 60!
A guide to help you make the most of the remaining years of your life

Instructions

This guidebook won't take long to read. It won't give you some incredible, mind-blowing new ideas that you probably haven't thought about before. What it will do is give you a concise list of suggestions you could do today to make the most of your remaining years of life.

This guidebook is designed for you to read and ponder the suggestions. Not all of them will be a fit for you, but I believe that many of them will be useful to you. I hope you then act on those that you feel will be beneficial to you. And the left hand page is intentionally left blank for you to make notes and jot down ideas while it's fresh in your mind.

After you've thought about which suggestions are appropriate for you, I suggest you re-read the guidebook a couple of weeks later. You'll make some corrections to the actions you are embarking on and perhaps you'll add or delete some of the suggestions to your "to do" list.

Time is of the essence. The sands of time are swiftly slipping down the hourglass of life. And you don't want to look back several years from now and feel you've not maximized your golden years. You can start living now – or you can let time erode these years. Doing nothing now is wasting the last few chapters of your life.

As you'll see, it's a quick read but I hope that you'll find it gives you motivation to make the most of your remaining years.

Chapter 1
Do the math

Holy Donkeys – you're over 60. Where did the time go?

We all know the answer to that question – the time went by as you lived life. School, working, dating while looking for a mate, finding a mate, raising a family, going on vacations, taking care of your parents, more working, more vacations, more weekends. And now you've hit the magical yet significant 60-year-old number. Holy Donkeys, where did the time go?

We can't rewind the clock – so what do we do? I like to tell myself; you are where you are, you can't change your history. But what you can do is to plan, shape and maximize your future. So, this book provides suggestions on how you can make the most of your remaining years on this earth. Not all my suggestions will be a match for you, but I do feel that many of them will be and if you act now, you can make your remaining years the best they can be – and even perhaps the best years of your life.

Let's look at statistics. If you're 60 today, your life expectancy is over 80 years. Yes, it varies by country, by gender, by lifestyle and a lot by genetics (how long and well did your parents live). But if you take 80 years as the baseline and then add (or subtract) for your specifics – then you'll have some idea (or target) of your longevity. Of course, we all know people who live well into their 90's, remaining active and sharp, but alas, we also know people who left this earth well before 80 due to a wide range of causes (cancer, accidents, etc.). With a guideline of 80 (again, your number will be different), you can see the urgency to make the most of your remaining years of your life.

The frustrating part is you don't know what your "number" will be or how you will be, physically or mentally, as you approach this number. We all want to be that superhuman that lives to 101, exercising every day and mentally sharp to the end. Or be the Betty White who lived to 99, actively working in show business well into her 90's. But you just don't know what your number will be, which provides even more incentive to make the most of today.

If you are 60 today, you have approximately a 60% chance of hitting 80 years of age if you are male or 70% chance if you are female. But the numbers drop as you reach 90 years old – with only ~20% of males hitting this number and 30% of females. And for the superhumans – low single digit chances of you hitting the magical mark of 100 years old.

My first suggestion is to break down your remaining years of life into decades. Your 60's, your 70's, your 80's and what the heck – let's dream and include the 90's. And if you hit 100, do whatever you can as soon as you can as, at that age, you are truly in the last chapter of life.

Suggestion #1: Break down your remaining years of life into decades – 60's, 70's, 80's and 90's.

Chapter 2
Make a written plan

When I hear a 25-year-old describe something as a "bucket list" trip, I chuckle to myself. What I would have labeled a bucket list trip when I was 25 years old is certainly different today. When I was 25, I might have called a super fun weekend at the beach with friends a bucket list item. But times, desires, finances, and responsibilities change but what doesn't change is time itself. I think it's imperative you create your own written plan and do it by decades (see Suggestion #1). And in this case, you may even want to be more specific, breaking it down by years or a couple of years.

And the "plan" isn't just about bucket list travel, your plan should include things such as learning to play the piano, learning French, honing your tennis game, read one of the classic novels each month, etc. Don't forget that many of these activities can help you both mentally and physically, as it's been proven that exercising the mind and body is crucial to not only extend your life but improve your quality of life.

This is an exercise that takes several weeks, if not longer. You'll want to create an initial draft, think it over, research options (and prices), talk it over with your significant other, sleep on it and make an updated version. Then rinse and repeat several times. It's not a static plan, as I encourage you to visit it every year or more frequently as things change. Your health may deteriorate/improve, and your responsibilities, finances, circumstances, and desires may change. But it's imperative you create a written plan, with goals and timing. If you don't, before you know it, you've hit another age milestone and perhaps missed something you can only enjoy as a younger person.

An example of a written plan could look something like this

Age 60	Take French for Travelers class at adult education center	$ 100
Age 60	2 weeks summer trip to France	$5,000
Age 60	Play in local tennis league	$ 50
Age 60	Take salsa dancing at local dance center	$ 250

Age 61	Read one classic novel per month (create a list of novels to read)	$ 100

Age 61	Volunteer at Meals on Wheels	$ 100
Age 61	Hike 7 days on Appalachian Trail in North Carolina	$ 1,000
Age 61	Take beginner piano classes at adult education center	$ 100
Age 62	Rent RV for 2 week USA road trip	$ 5,000
Age 62	AirBnB rental for 1 week in Northern Georgia	$ 2,000
Age 62	Volunteer at local hospital	$ 10
Age 62	Teach grandson how to play gin rummy	$ 10

As I mentioned, this is a dynamic list that the first

draft will take a couple of weeks to create and then you'll modify it frequently as you not only accomplish your goals but also modify it as things change in your life. It's important you create one as it would be quite easy to get into the routine of life and before you know it – you are several years/decades older. Some of you may only create one or two goals for each year and some of you may create a complex yearly list with many entries. I stress that your goals need to be very detailed with specific timing, otherwise, if you just have general goals, they become easy to brush off, postpone or ignore.

At the end of the book, I've put in Appendix A a blank workbook to help you get started with your written plan. It's a suggested format, your actual one may be different, including a section for notes, etc. It can really be in any format you want, as long as you write it down with the specific actions and timing.

Suggestion #2: Create a detailed, written plan of things you want to accomplish with specific timing and dates. Review and modify it frequently.

Chapter 3
Attitude

We all know a Mr. or Ms. Grumpy. We may have had a mother, father, neighbor, or friend who became grumpy as they got older. As a result, people tended to avoid them and talk about them behind their backs. Grandkids would ask their mom or dad, "why is Grandpa so grumpy"? Of course, you may have even vowed never to be that way when you got older. Okay, now that you are older – are you beginning to develop a grumpier personality?

My theory – it's all about attitude. It's easy to slowly slide into a negative attitude. Perhaps some difficult live event (illness, loss of a loved one, etc.) makes you depressed and you don't make the effort to overcome the situation. You might not realize it, but day by day you incrementally change into this new but undesired personality. You may have been fun and the life of the party in your younger days. Then one day you suddenly realize (or even worse, be told) that you've become quite grumpy with a negative attitude, or as my sister says, quite the curmudgeon.

If you have become this person, you can change. But it's not easy to do. It's far easier to make the conscious effort not to go down that slippery slope towards this negative attitude before you get to that stage.

But how do I avoid becoming Mr. Grumpy?

First, stay mentally young. We all know the 95-year-old friend who is up for just about anything. They're fun, energetic and look on the positive side. They are not afraid to try new things, new styles and make a conscious effort to be young – or dare I say "hip". In other words, don't be a stick in the mud. Don't act old but be young at heart, mind, and body (as much as you can).

Secondly, quit bitching. Life has been and always will be full of trials and tribulations. Someone is going to cut you off in traffic, miss an appointment with you, be late or forget to do something for you. Don't waste your time and energy complaining about it. Focus on your end zone – what you want to get done and move on. Spending time whining about it doesn't get you to your end zone – you just end up getting more frustrated over the "injustice" you incurred.

Also, pick your battles. Not every injustice should be dismissed. Some you may actually need to make it known that something is wrong. What I'm saying is pick which battle you want to fight. Don't fight a battle that the outcome won't make a difference. If complaining about it will help resolve it – go for it. If not, move on.

All of us will have a decline in our cognitive abilities as we age. Our 60+ year old brain processes events more slowly than our 20 year our brain. We'll have trouble multi-tasking and will occasionally forget things, lose a train of thought, or can't remember the movie we watched last night. But keeping a positive, upbeat attitude when these things happen will help keep you from becoming Mr. Grumpy. My mother, in her later stages of life, had begun to have an increased loss of cognitive ability and memory. I'd ask her what she had for breakfast, and she'd just laugh and say, "I have no idea if I even had breakfast", chuckling to herself. Though I was sad she could not remember very short-term memories, I smiled as she kept up a positive, fun attitude.

I unfortunately had a relative who became quite negative and aggressive as her cognitive abilities declined with age. She would complain about everything, nothing was ever right and even complained to her husband one day that he brought her the afternoon glass of milk in the wrong type of glass. Her negative attitude only worsened her condition, and she became more reclusive. Sadly, she withdrew from everyday activities and conversations. And worse, people (including family) tended to limit their time with her as it just wasn't a pleasant conversation or experience. I'm convinced this negative attitude accelerated her mental/physical decline. You really want to keep the upbeat personality that make friends and family gravitate to you.

Years ago, a colleague of mine was describing a party he had just been to, describing the fun everyone had enjoyed. I made the comment to him, "Sounds like your best party ever!". He quickly replied, "No way, I want to keep the attitude that I've not had my best party/time/experience yet – that it's still to come". I thought about his comment and felt he was spot on. Don't think that you'll never have fun again, you won't have a great time. Yes, you might not be dancing on tables, but you can live with the attitude that you haven't had your best time ever – that's it still to come.

We all know what kind of person we want to be in our later years of life – but you have to work at it daily. It won't happen automatically, you have to make a conscious and determined effort to be a positive elder versus the Mr. or Ms. Grumpy. I encourage you to start each day with a reminder that you have a choice – be upbeat and positive that day or let negativity ruin your day.

Suggestion #3: Stay mentally young, making a conscious effort to stay positive and upbeat. Remind yourself each morning you have a choice of what you'll be that day – positive while enjoying the day or negative and let it ruin your day.

Suggestion #4: Don't waste your time complaining about perceived injustices – move on towards your end zone.

Suggestion #5: Pick your battles. If you do have to complain about an injustice – make sure it's one that your complaining will make a difference. If not, move on,

Suggestion #6: Live life as if your best time ever is still to come.

Chapter 4
Health & Exercise

There are thousands of books, blogs and websites on senior health and exercise. I'm not going to list diets, menus or guidelines on healthy eating and exercising. What I am going to list are some basic facts that we all know but are helpful to remind ourselves from time to time.

Health. As they say, taking care of your health is the most important thing you can do to help yourself live long and maximize your enjoyment of your remaining years of life. Getting regular checkups, taking your prescribed medicines, and watching your weight are all key ingredients to maximizing your longevity. Check your blood pressure frequently, check your blood sugar periodically and follow your doctor's advice. And if you've not had a medical checkup lately, do so now. Modern medicine is one of the ways to extend your life, both in years and quality.

Exercise. Okay, we're not going to win Wimbledon now that we're over 60. We're not going to beat 20-year-old runners in marathons. But it has been proven over and over that regular, daily exercise of some fashion is instrumental in improving your health, maintaining a healthy weight, keeping strong bone density and muscle tone. All these benefits are attainable by any of us – it just takes discipline to do something every day. And "something" doesn't have to be running 5 miles a day but can be as simple as walking around the block several times. You must pick what daily exercises you can do, find enjoyable and have the discipline to do them frequently.

Exercise is good for body and mind. And it's been proven that exercise will help you fall asleep quicker and improves sleep quality. Studies have shown that moderate aerobic exercise increases the amount of deep sleep one has each night. Everyone is different, but experts advise not to exercise close to bedtime as it can take time for your brain to wind down and your body to cool down.

Age related muscle loss. Despite your feeling that you're a "higher species" and you don't suffer from age related muscle loss, all of us started losing muscle mass after the age of 30. It's a fact of life. But preventing the decline (and even increasing your muscle mass) helps you delay the aging process, improves balance and is part of a healthy daily regime. Strengthening your core muscles help you maintain good balance while reducing the chance of a fall.

It comes down to motivation and discipline. You have to find what motivates you to keep the discipline of daily exercises. Perhaps it's one of your target goals – let's say, to hike the Alps. You know you need to train for 3 months, so it's this goal that provides the motivation for you to achieve and maximize the enjoyment of the goal. Find your own motivational idea to maintain the discipline.

And of course, I add the legal disclaimer, if you're

new to exercising, check with your doctor before embarking on any new exercise regimen.

Suggestion #7: Work at a healthy diet and lifestyle. Do some form of exercise daily. It will help you maximize (and lengthen) the remaining years of your life.

Chapter 5
Music

This chapter is truly music to one's ear. In our younger days, music was probably frequently played in your room, car, apartment, on a date, etc. Music would have given you great joy back then, as you would listen to songs and connect them to fun and positive experiences. But as we grew older and matured, got jobs, had kids, listened to 24-hour news – music probably was played less and less in your life.

If this is the case, you need to revert to your younger self. Listening to music (or even better, playing it yourself) has been scientifically proven by multiple studies to be a mood enhancer, fight off depression, relieve stress, improve sleep quality, and help release pleasure causing substances in the brain. Music can put you in a good place mentally, especially if you're doing boring and tedious tasks. And music has been proven to activate almost all brain regions and networks

Unless you're a serious music aficionado, don't bother buying CD's or albums. The average person today uses a streaming service. There are several options, Spotify, Amazon Music, and Apple Music are perhaps the most well-known and are super easy to use. If you're wondering which service is best for you, ask your son/daughter as they will certainly be using one of these streaming services.

I recommend creating multiple playlists to have

ready for various occasions. For instance, some of my playlists are "Cruising the Bahama's", "Sunday Morning" and "Cocktail Party". That way, if I want some background music for a party on a Friday night, I can select my "Cocktail Party" playlist. Or if I'm grilling on my back patio on a Saturday summer evening, I might queue up my "Cruising the Bahama's" playlist. And some songs might be on several playlists. It's yours to create, add, or delete as you want.

Don't limit yourself to what you listened to when you were 20. Add current songs as it will help you look and feel younger (or dare I say more "hip"). I have my 32-year-old daughter send me song recommendations that her generation is listening to and many of them I add to my playlists. So, when I'm talking to the younger crowd, I can drop in the name of a current song, impressing them with my "hipster" status.

Suggestion #8: Bring music back into your life. Create specific playlists and let music enhance your day.

Chapter 6
Travel

This chapter is intertwined with the first 2 chapters, but I highlight it as it's such an important topic. Hopefully you've created your master plan of things you want to do by certain ages. And you've revised it multiple times and will continue to do so over your lifetime.

Have you seen the Expedia commercial with Ewan McGregor? It really is a great commercial as he surmises that as you reflect on your life, you won't wish you had bought more "stuff" but had traveled to more of the places you want to go. He asks the question, "Do you really need a smarter, smart phone or a thinner, thin TV?" Which to me is spot on – unless you're a billionaire, you only have so much disposable income. Think carefully on what you want to spend it on. More stuff or more travel?

Studies have shown that travel is good for your mind as well. It can lower the risk of depression, reduce stress, increase satisfaction, improve happiness, and stimulates the brain. Additionally, planning for a big trip is part of the fun as well, as you research, plan, and organize your trip. It's easy today to do so much pre-planning on where to go, where to stay, activities to do and I strongly believe that this planning of your trip is a significant portion of the enjoyment of your travel experience.

My sister had a friend who was an avid traveler, but

in her later years had developed a serious illness, making her unable to travel. So instead, she then watched hundreds of travel shows on places she had been and places she wanted to go as a substitute to actually traveling. This virtual travel experience allowed her to still enjoy "traveling" though she no longer could.

I also encourage you to think about what travel you can do in your 60's versus 70's versus 80's. Want to hike the Alps? You might be able to do it in your 70's, but more than likely, you'll enjoy it most at an earlier age. Perhaps save the England Garden tour until later and tackle your wanderlust for more physical travel earlier in your 60's.

Suggestion #9: Prioritize your travel based upon physicality requirements versus your age. And think carefully – do you need more stuff or more experiences?

Chapter 7
Friends

It's been scientifically proven that keeping an active social life as we age is good for the mind and body. But like everything else I've discussed so far in this book, it's something you have to work at to keep it active with you. Many things in life can diminish your desire to remain socially active – an illness, death of a spouse, retirement or reduced hearing or sight. So, it's important that you work at keeping an active social life. According to one study, people with strong social connections have substantially higher odds of outliving those who have fewer social connections.

Research has also shown that people who are socially active with friends and family can improve their immune system, help them recover more quickly from illness, sharpen their memory, and even help them live a longer life. Friends and family can also help you keep your health on track, encouraging you to remain socially active and maintain your regular Doctor's visits, checkups, and exams.

If you are one of those people with an extensive network of friends that you are actively engaged with, good for you. But if you're not, this is an area you really need to work on. We all know it's sometimes hard to meet new people. Some of the things you can do to meet new people is to volunteer for an organization, take an adult learning class, join a gym or other organized activities that will give you a chance to make new friends.

If you're newly single by either a divorce or death of your spouse, meeting new potential mates may be especially challenging. Studies have shown that married couples have longer life expectancies and better health than their single counterparts. There is always an exception to this, but in general, having a partner in life improves many of the things we need in our golden years. Help when you get sick, someone to enjoy the special moments with and someone to be there when you need them. So, if you're newly single, there are many dating sites which allow you to input a desired age range, traits, and likes/dislike. And some dating sites cater specifically to seniors, such as Silver Singles, Senior Match or Our Time. Often there are local dating sites for towns that make it easier to find a nearby potential mate.

Suggestion # 10. Remain socially active, it's been proven to be a huge health and mental benefit. If you're not socially active, get involved with activities which will allow you to meet new friends.

Chapter 8
Sex

As I don't think teenagers will be rushing out to read this book, I can address the "S" word – Sex. And nicely done if you're one of those people who, while scanning the list of chapters in the beginning and saw a chapter titled "Sex", and immediately flipped to this page. In this case, you might not need this chapter's suggestions.

When we were in our 20's and 30's, sex was frequently on your mind. And depending on your relationship status, it was probably frequently happening. Then kids came, work increased, and a wide range of responsibilities ramped up and before you knew it, you were over 60 and sex was happening less and less.

Now that you're over 60, your sex frequency may have really decreased. Once a week? Once a month? Rarely ever? More than likely, you're having sex much less than you had in your younger days, so how do you change this trend?

In our young adulthood years, sex was easy. A quickie before a dinner party, a late-night session after a movie or a weekend morning wakeup call with one another. But as we age, spontaneity isn't as easy. Our libido isn't as strong, we tire quickly and after a glass or two of wine, you might really prefer to watch the latest Netflix show. You might also have health issues which reduce your drive/ability to have sex. This guide isn't a substitute for medical evaluation or advice, but it hopefully will give you some ideas on how to increase and improve your sex. Of course, if you've not been active sexually in recent years, check with your medical professional first.

We've all heard on the numerous television commercials that there are lots of prescriptions that may help the many men with erectile dysfunction.

The good news on the prescription front is many of the patents on Viagra and Cialis have expired, which means they are now much more affordable from a variety of reputable web sites.

So how do you increase and improve your sexual activities? I encourage you to plan it, schedule it and as I like to say "orchestrate" your sex. Otherwise, if you don't, things will come up, you'll be too busy watching your favorite show, making dinner, or watching the grandkids.

When I say orchestrate it, I mean just that. Tell your partner that "tomorrow let's plan for some "fun" (my code word for sex) after our lunch on Saturday. Then keep the TV off, put on some fun music and then enjoy one another. But if you don't schedule it, you can't orchestrate it. And if you don't schedule it, more than likely something else will take priority. *Remember, sex really is the spice of life.*

Suggestion #11: Schedule/Orchestrate your sexual activities. If you don't, something else will take their place.

Chapter 9
Memories

If we look back on our life, we have a trove of memories. Some of the memories are only in our mind and some of them we have physical reminders of them. We have post cards, ticket stubs and lots and lots of pictures. We may even have 35mm slides from "back in the day" and old photos in boxes in the attic. Of course, today we do everything digitally, storing hundreds (or maybe even thousands) on our phones and computers. Whether it's photos in a box in the attic or digitally stored photos, I would argue that you rarely go back and look at them.

So why don't you go back and relive these memories? I would suggest it's because they're not organized in a manner that is easy and convenient for you to take a stroll down memory lane. It's not readily available, they're not organized by vacation or phases of life. They're just thrown into boxes, drawers or a huge photo folder on your phone or computer.

For me, I don't find myself sitting at my computer and scrolling through all my photos. Many of us still like the physical feel of a real book. What I suggest is to create digitally prepared photo books of specific events, whether it's a book of your daughters' younger years, your annual family vacations to Sea Island or a collage of Christmas's. Today's way to create these books is super easy. You select the online company/service you want to use (I use Shutterfly but there are many other services), upload your photos, organize them in your desired sequence, and add any captions you desire. A week later, the finished book appears in your mailbox. It's that easy.

After a month in the Alps last summer with family, my sister kindly created a Shutterfly book showing off photos and captions of our grand adventure. It's a wonderful keepsake that I find myself fondly looking at time and time again. And this past January, I spent two weeks skiing in Switzerland with family. Upon my return, I promptly went online and created a photobook from the hundreds of photos we took while over there. I now have a physical hard copy photo book of my memories from this skiing trip. I can sit on the couch and relive my trip while enjoying a glass of wine. It really is a wonderful and easy way to relieve your memories. So, pick whichever company you will use – and create a memory book. No, let me change that – create many memory books.

And as we age even older, we won't be glued to our computers as much as we are today. When my mother was in her late 80's, her memory was fading. But we had created several picture books of life events and her favorite trips, and she would sit on the couch fondly being able to enjoy her memories. They not only gave her pleasure in recalling the event, but we felt it was helping her to work her memory brain cells to think back to those days. She certainly wasn't in the mindful state to use a computer but to sit there and flip through a picture book was a healthy and easy experience for her. If you create your memory books now, you'll not only enjoy them today – but have them for your enjoyment much later in life. But you must do it today – while you have the time and drive to do so.

And these memory books don't have to be all pictures. They can be a scrapbook of postcards of places you've been, ticket stubs from events you've attended or even cocktail napkins from various hotels/resorts/restaurants you've been to. It doesn't matter what the physical reminder is - but it's important to put it in a book that allows you to enjoy that trip or phase of life over and over.

Suggestion #12: Create memory books that you can enjoy today – but will really be beneficial as you age.

Chapter 10
Declutter

For 60 years, you've been accumulating "stuff". Your parents probably saved various items from your early childhood, you might have your high school yearbooks, love letters from your spouse and most likely you inherited some furniture from your parents when they passed on. You might have an attic full of boxes with things you've not looked at for years.

Now I'm not saying you've become a hoarder, but I might suggest you have more stuff than you need or haven't used in a very long time. I am a big believer if you haven't used something in the past year, you probably don't need it. Now is the time to declutter your house and your lifestyle. There are dozens of websites with decluttering tips to help give you ideas. My suggestion is to tackle this project in small bites, perhaps one room a weekend.

I also believe that decluttering now is beneficial when you have a life changing event. If you have to move to an assisted living facility, you'll be a step ahead as you've decluttered years ago. And when you do die, your kids will thank you for not having to get rid of 40 years of National Geographics or the dozens of empty gallon milk jugs you've stashed in the attic (as my father did). And by giving away some of your treasures to your kids now, you're letting them enjoy that heirloom while you're still around.

I have a friend that every New Year's Day, hangs

all of her clothes so that the hangers are all pointed the same way. Then when she wears one of the items during the year, she puts it back in her closet with the hanger pointing the other way. Then the next New Year's Day, any clothes that she hasn't worn (by noting which hangers had not been turned around), she donates them to charity or takes them to a consignment store. An excellent idea in my opinion.

Suggestion # 13: Declutter today, while you can. Take small bites at this project, perhaps a room per weekend, keeping only things that you've used in the past year.

Chapter 11
Just in case

We've all known or heard of people who became critically or gravely ill and were no longer able to make their own health care decisions. The medical experts then have to rely upon family members to make the medical decisions on what or what not to do to extend their life. And if you've not specifically told your family what you want done to extend (or not extend) your life, you are placing a heavy burden on them. Even worse, some of your family may want one course of action and others a different one, creating a very tense situation that could cause angst among them for many years.

So, just in case the worst-case scenario happens, don't you want your family to know your wishes and desires rather than guess? It varies by state or country, but the most common way to let your loved ones know your medical wishes is with a document like a living will, advanced directive or a 5 wishes document. These are legal documents that detail, very specifically, what kind and extent of medical actions should be taken when you are no longer able to make these decisions.

This is a sensitive subject but one that I feel is quite important. For me, if I'm no longer able to speak, get out of a bed and be mentally or physically active, I don't want my family to do whatever it takes to extend my life. The physical, emotional, and financial toll it takes on a family is enormous. So, to protect them, I've gotten a legal living will which expresses my wishes. Just in case.

And while we're on the subject of "just in case", I would encourage you to consider being an organ donor should the worst happen. This, too, is a sensitive topic, but one that might save someone else's life. My sister and I joke, they might not want our livers (too many happy hours) but of course they want our brains (this is when the jokes really start). But joking aside, I encourage you to become an organ donor. It varies state by state, but in the State of Florida, it's a simple notation on your driver's license.

Suggestion # 14. Create a living will, advanced directive or 5 wishes document. And consider being an organ donor. Your loved ones will thank you.

Chapter 12
D-Day Planning

Of course, I'm not talking about the courageous landing of Allied troops for the World War II D-Day invasion in France, I'm referring to your personal D-Day – the day you pass on.

Many of you don't want to think about it, telling yourself you'll just let your kids sort out your stuff after you're gone. Thinking or planning for your D-Day isn't something that you have any desire to do – or worse, something you keep postponing, thinking you've got the time to do it later. But as we know, we never know if we will have a year's notice of our D-Day, a month or whether it arrives tonight with no notice.

I had a friend whose last parent died suddenly with zero D-Day planning. His father refused to talk about finances, where his will was, where he kept his money, etc., telling him that he would give him the details later. Then a heart attack took his life overnight and my friend was stuck combing through stacks and stacks of paper records to find where things were kept (his father was a borderline paper hoarder). He had to try and create a list of accounts, passwords, and details. He literally was looking in books, under beds and behind pictures for any documents. He even found $200 in travelers checks (remember those?) in an old suitcase. And his father left no details on his final wishes – to be buried or cremated, where to bury him, etc.

My friend loved his father dearly, but more than once he lamented the fact that because his father did not plan for his D-Day, he spent countless hours and expense figuring out the details. He had to make final burial decisions not knowing his father's desires. My friend is convinced he's not found all his father's assets as they were not organized for retrieval. He also second guesses the final wishes he executed for his father – wondering if that is what his father would have wanted.

I encourage you to formalize your final wishes. Write down if you want to be buried or cremated. Document if you want a big memorial service, graveside service or a celebration of life party. I know people who have selected what songs they want played at their service. I personally have written down where I want my ashes spread and have included plastic tubes (with caps) in my "In case of death" folder for them to put some of my ashes to take to the various places to spread them. You want to document all the details so that when that fateful day does arrive, your family knows exactly what to do with the knowledge and comfort that they're doing what you want them to do. And the more detailed your final wishes are, the easier it is on your grieving family. A word of warning: Have a box of tissues handy while you're documenting your final wishes. You're more than likely to get a bit teary eyed completing it (I know I did). It's perhaps one of the most important decisions you'll make – and one that will be for eternity.

Lastly on this topic, keep all of this information in one location that you and key people in your family know where it is. As mentioned, I have an "In case of death" folder that I keep all my D Day material in – will, final wishes, plastic test tubes for my ashes, etc. Don't make them go on an Easter Egg hunt trying to find your final wishes when your D-Day happens.

To help you get started, below is a list of topics that, at a minimum, should be considered and documented for your next of kin to handle.

-Burial or Cremation
-If buried, where
-If cremated, what to do with your ashes
-Type of service or a celebration of life party
-Specific requests for your service/party
-Location of your will or trust documents
-List of bank/stock accounts/credit cards
-List of passwords
-Location of important items (car titles, keys, etc.)
-Safety deposit box details/key, if applicable
-Hiding spots where you keep valuables in the house

Suggestion #15: Please, plan for your D-Day. Document your final wishes - the more detailed, the better. Let your next of kin know where your D-Day documents are kept. Your kids and heirs will thank you.

Chapter 13
Once you have passed

As I've stressed numerous times in this guidebook, you never know when your D-Day will occur, hence it's so important to make your plans now. But I also encourage you to create some reminders of yourself now that you can keep for your friends and family to discover after D-Day.

Specifically, I encourage you to write letters to people who are significant to you. I have letters written to my wife and 2 daughters and placed them in my "In case of death" folder. They haven't seen them and won't until I'm gone – but in them I write about fond memories specific to each of them. That way while they're grieving my passing, they will have some comfort in knowing how much I enjoyed those special times. And as time goes by, I've periodically updated the letters adding in recent memories that were significant to me. I would also bet that they'll keep these letters for the rest of their life as a special keepsake from me.

It doesn't only have to be for your immediate family. Dean Smith, the late former head basketball coach of the University of North Carolina, left instructions in his will to give each of his former players $200 with the note to "have dinner on Coach Smith". No one knew Coach Smith was going to do this until he had passed, but I'm guessing it made a lasting and fond memory for his players. Talk about sending a final farewell from his grave. Brilliant. Just a brilliant idea.

I also encourage you to leave various items or notes hidden in places that people most likely won't find until your passing. Perhaps you put a note under your shirts in a dresser. Or put a picture with comments on it in a folder that only you go into now but know your family will when you pass. You might also put various notes in desk drawers or how about taking Coach Dean Smith's idea – put some money in an envelope addressed to a loved one with the message inside "Have dinner on me" and put it somewhere that they'll discover after your D-Day. What you are giving them is a "visitation" from you after you've passed. And a fond and pleasant memory has been created.

Unless you're famous, your life and personality won't be remembered once the last generation of your kids or grandkids who knew you has passed. So, it's important that you help keep your memory alive with these simple but effective "visitations" for your family to enjoy when you're gone. Recently, we gave my oldest daughter her baby memorabilia (yes, we were decluttering!). Inside this box was the local newspaper from the day she was born with a note from her deceased grandfather, welcoming her to this world. It was a special "visitation" from her beloved grandfather well after he had passed.

Suggestion #16: Leave letters (updated as years go

by) and other "hidden" surprises for your loved ones for them to discover after your D-Day.

Summary

Suggestion #1: Break down your remaining years of life into decades – 60's, 70's, 80's and 90's.

Suggestion #2: Create a detailed, written plan of things you want to accomplish with specific timing and dates. Review and modify it frequently.

Suggestion #3: Stay mentally young, making a conscious effort to stay positive and upbeat. Remind yourself each morning you have a choice of what you'll be that day – positive while enjoying the day or negative and let it ruin your day.

Suggestion #4: Don't waste your time complaining about perceived injustices – move on towards your end zone.

Suggestion #5: Pick your battles. If you do have to complain about an injustice – make sure it's one that your complaining will make a difference. If not, move on.

Suggestion #6: Live life that your best time ever is still to come.

Suggestion #7: Work at a healthy diet and lifestyle. Do some form of exercise daily. It will help you maximize (and lengthen) the remaining years of your life.

Suggestion #8: Bring music back into your life. Create specific playlists and let music enhance your day.

Suggestion #9: Prioritize your travel based upon physicality requirements vs your age. And think carefully – do you need more stuff or more experiences?

Suggestion # 10. Remain socially active, it's been proven to be a huge health and mental benefit. If you're not socially active, get involved with activities which will allow you to meet new friends.

Suggestion #11: Schedule/Orchestrate your sexual activities. If you don't, something else will take their place.

Suggestion #12: Create memory books that you can enjoy today – but will really be beneficial as you age.

Suggestion # 13: Declutter today, while you can. Take small bites at this project, perhaps a room per weekend, keeping only things that you've used in the past year.

Suggestion # 14. Create a living will, advanced

directive or 5 wishes document. And consider being an organ donor. Your loved ones will thank you.

Suggestion #15: Please, plan for your D-Day. Document your final wishes, the more detailed, the better. Let your next of kin know where your D-Day documents are kept. Your kids and heirs will thank you.

Suggestion #16: Leave letters (updated as years go by) and other "hidden" surprises for your loved ones for them to discover after your D-Day.

In Closing

As promised, this wasn't a long book to read. And no earth-shattering ideas were revealed. But it is a guidebook of suggestions that if you implement some of them, will help you make the most of your remaining years of your life. I also encourage you to re-read this guidebook from time to time, to refresh and reinforce these suggestions.

I started out this book with two sayings. The first:

I plan on living forever, so far, so good

Well, if you're reading this right now, you're right, you are continuing to live – so far, so good. But we all know that we'll have our D-Day, but we just don't know when it will be.

Which brings me to my second saying at the beginning of the book:

Tempus Fugit, so Carpe Diem

Time Flies so Seize the Day, a loose translation of two Latin phrases. I truly feel this should be your motto once you are over 60. Time is flying by – so don't wait – make the most of your remaining years of your life.

Thanks for reading this. I hope this guidebook encourages you to take action on some of the suggestions. But don't wait – do it today!

The End

About the Author

This is Mayson Brooks' first book, and the idea came to him over several adult beverages one evening.

A graduate of the US Naval Academy, after 6 years on active duty sailing the high seas, he had a 30 year career in the semiconductor industry.

He splits his time between Sarasota, Florida; Zermatt, Switzerland and St Barths, French West Indies. He is indeed, over 60 – Holy Donkeys!

www.HolyDonkeys.com

www.ingramcontent.com/pod-product-compliance
Lightning Source LLC
LaVergne TN
LVHW020134080526
838201LV00119B/3841